Mature Bird Care

Delia Berlin

© T.F.H. Publications, Inc.

Distributed in the UNITED STATES to the Pet Trade by T.F.H. Publications, Inc., 1 TFH Plaza, Neptune City, NJ 07753; on the Internet at www.tfh.com; in CANADA by Rolf C. Hagen Inc., 3225 Sartelon St., Montreal, Quebec H4R 1E8; Pet Trade by H & L Pet Supplies Inc., 27 Kingston Crescent, Kitchener, Ontario N2B 2T6; in ENGLAND by T.F.H. Publications, PO Box 74, Havant PO9 5TT; in AUSTRALIA AND THE SOUTH PACIFIC by T.F.H. (Australia), Pty. Ltd., Box 149, Brookvale 2100 N.S.W., Australia; in NEW ZEALAND by Brooklands Aquarium Ltd., 5 McGiven Drive, New Plymouth, RD1 New Zealand; in SOUTH AFRICA by Rolf C. Hagen S.A. (PTY.) LTD., P.O. Box 201199, Durban North 4016, South Africa; in Japan by T.F.H. Publications. Published by T.F.H. Publications, Inc.

Manufactured in the
United States of America
by T.F.H. Publications, Inc.

Contents

Introduction

This book provides information about caring for mature pet birds, more specifically, caring for mature parrots. Here, "parrot" refers to any bird in the parrot family, which includes birds as diverse as parakeets and macaws. Parrots share certain characteristics, among them a set of very "handy" feet (with two toes pointing forward and two backwards) and a strong, hooked bill. Almost every other physical characteristic of parrots, from size to color, can vary tremendously from species to species.

Most parrots have something else in common that has made them favorite companions for centuries: a highly intelligent and social nature. These characteristics, coupled with long life spans and the potential to produce human speech sounds, have made parrots true family members in many households around the world. Unfortunately, these same characteristics, in combination with their ability to inflict painful bites, produce loud noise, and destroy furnishings, contribute to a high rate of pet parrot displacements. Most of these negative behaviors appear as the bird matures without proper socialization. Well-meaning pet owners, who usually acquired the bird as a baby, and with little or no information, are often so disappointed and frustrated by these behaviors that they decide to give up their bird.

Though most of the information provided here applies to pet birds in general, the emphasis is on mature birds. What exactly is a "mature" bird? In this book, we refer to a bird as mature when it has reached breeding age. This age varies with species, and it tends to increase with the size of the bird. A cockatiel, for example, may be able to breed before two years of age, while an African Grey parrot may start producing young at the age of five. However, once birds reach this stage, they undergo hormonal changes that result in some changes in appearance and behavior. These changes have an impact on proper care and training practices. The same bird that was always gentle may act aggressively near his favorite swing. The pet that went along with any visitors may start biting guests.

You may have noticed that most birds for sale at pet stores, parrots in particular, are very young. These young "baby" birds are highly trainable and will bond easily to caretakers. However, like children, they come equipped with individual personalities, and their human "parents" may socialize them properly or reinforce bad habits. As a consequence, when pet birds mature and lose their submissiveness, many owners become disappointed and disinterested in their previously sweet, cuddly companion. These changes may require adjustments in expectations and some new strategies, but they don't need to result in loss of affection or tragic separation.

A bird's behavior may change as it matures, but the proper socialization and training can help ensure a long and rewarding relationship.

Does this mean that a mature bird will no longer be affectionate? Not at all. With proper guidance and consistent good care, pet birds can be the most rewarding long-time companions.

Although baby birds may bond to an owner more easily than an older bird, there are many advantages to owning a mature bird.

Even birds that have a history of abuse and longstanding neglect can develop fulfilling relationships with new owners.

In addition, mature birds often develop very desirable characteristics, such as a more steady temperament. Like older children, they tend to become quieter in their play and therefore less prone to injuries and accidents. Their experience with a variety of situations over time tends to make them less flighty and more self-confident. And if they have had the good fortune to establish solid bonds with their caretakers, they become more trustworthy and loyal companions.

If you have had a bird for a long time and have become disenchanted or disinterested, this book can help you revitalize and improve your relationship with your pet. If you are thinking of getting a new pet bird, this book may help you consider opening your home to an older bird in need of a good home. Pet birds will flourish in good hands and will let you know that they appreciate your responsible care.

Realistic Expectations

Nothing entertains a pet bird more than social interaction and companionship. Reciprocally, most responsible pet owners enjoy their interaction with their pets. Why have a pet that requires significant daily care and expense if its company is not enjoyable? With this in mind, you can make the most of your relationship by planning your environment and daily routines to maximize positive interaction with your pet.

Birds are very long-lived, and because most people lead very busy lives, a routine that will demand most of your free time will burn you out quickly. Birds are creatures of habit, so doing a lot with your bird for awhile and losing interest later will cause a great deal of suffering to your pet. Because birds don't tend to suffer in silence, your quality of life also will be affected when your bird is unhappy. Screaming, biting, plucking, destructive chewing, and self-mutilation are some of the habits that neglected birds develop in frustration.

Does your lifestyle allow for the commitment that caring for a pet bird calls for? To answer this question affirmatively, you must be able to integrate a minimum of three hours of bird-related activities into your day without undue stress for you and your family. These three hours don't need to involve exclusive attention to your bird. For example, you can take your bird out of its cage in the morning and, after an affectionate greeting and a good breakfast, read the paper with your bird nearby. After this, an appropriate swing installed in the back of your bathtub may allow you to share your morning shower with your bird. If you work, upon returning home you may give your bird a treat on a playpen within view of your working area while you fix dinner. After supper, cleaning and servicing the cage while talking, whistling, or singing with your bird can provide light exercise and stress release for both of you. Reading or watching the news side by side, a bedtime cuddle or a few head scratches may be appropriate ways to end each day.

Parrots are very social creatures that require a good deal of interaction, whether it is a ride on your shoulder, a shared evening meal, or a morning shower.

Depending on your lifestyle, a different routine may better suit you, but you will need to find the time and inclination to provide your bird with social company and proper husbandry on a daily basis, hopefully, for a very long time.

What About Talking?

Consider your expectations about pet ownership. Unfortunately, many novice pet parrot owners are seduced by the prospects of having a talking bird. Although a bird that talks often becomes the source of much amusement and conversation, talking is unpredictable and just one of many special qualities that a bird may have. Even when birds do talk, most fail to do so on command or in the company of strangers. Each bird is a unique living being that should be respected as such. The pre-existing expectation that a parrot should talk is frequently a source of disappointment and may get in the way of establishing a good relationship.

If talking is important to you, an advantage of getting a mature bird is that the talking potential already has been established. A mature parrot that never talked is not very likely to start talking, while a mature parrot that is a good talker is unlikely to stop. There are exceptions to this rule, however. Many pet owners who open their homes to an unwanted bird are happily surprised when

African Greys and Amazons are known for their talking ability; these chatterboxes learn better at a younger age but can continue throughout their life.

they first hear the bird talking. In the previous situation the bird may have been depressed, may have lacked the attention and stimulation to talk, or may have even been talking but nobody noticed due to neglect. Similarly, some very good talkers at times decide to abandon certain phrases and words for unknown reasons.

Parrot Love

Another expectation that people tend to have of pets in general is that they will provide some form of physical affection. It is important to realize that the behaviors that symbolize affection for humans are those behaviors that are used to express affection among humans. These behaviors may not be natural or acceptable for other species. Likewise, a human may not like being profusely licked or sniffed by a dog, even though that is the dog's way of expressing affection. Understanding the natural social behaviors of animals and respecting their specific needs can go a long way toward establishing a trusting and rewarding relationship.

What are the natural social behaviors of a mature parrot? A parrot is a prey animal and as such is constantly on the alert for potential dangers. Eyes strategically placed on the sides of the head can monitor ground and sky at the same time. Anything approaching from above is likely to be life threatening, so all parrots are naturally wary about having their backs touched. Although very tame parrots allow their owners to pet them on the back, this contact should never be forced or rushed because it reinforces natural fears.

Mutual preening of feathers is a natural behavior in flocks, so humans can look forward to gently petting the heads of their parrots in ways that simulate preening. Different types of parrots have different types of feathers, and therefore different preening preferences, but the best way of learning the "correct" way of preening your bird is to move slowly and gently while observing the bird's reactions.

Another common behavior of mature parrots involves regurgitation of food to close floc members, as an expression of affection or in greeting. Though this may not seem particularly appealing, a parrot bobbing its head up and

Although preening is a natural behavior for birds, some do not enjoy being petted by their owners.

Learn to recognize your parrot's body language: the Amazon is relaxed on the left and alert on the right.

down as it struggles to bring up a bit of semi-digested food is expressing affection. This rarely involves large amounts of regurgitate, but if this is too repulsive to you, a different type of pet may better suit you.

Peace and Quiet?

Noise production is another natural behavior of parrots. It can be curbed or modified, but not eliminated. A healthy parrot must vocalize some every day. Because people have different levels of tolerance for noise, subjective descriptions are often useless. Make sure you hear a bird's vocalizations firsthand before deciding if it is the right bird for you.

Obedience?

Another characteristic we may expect from our pets is obedience. If obedience comes high on your list of expected behaviors, a parrot may not be the best pet for you. Few parrots like to do things on command, or simply to please their owners. In addition, even those that do things on command do so much less reliably than a dog. Although obedience is not related to intelligence, it is related to the type of norms that animals use in their natural groups in the wild. A pack of dogs is more hierarchical in organization than a flock of parrots, so dogs are more inclined to submit to their superiors.

This is not to say that parrots will always rule the house. Certainly, many parrots and their owners live happy lives in harmony with each other. However, in general, there is little predictability about training outcomes with parrots. The parrot you plan to train to talk and ride on your shoulder may end up being a pet that doesn't talk but whistles, and that doesn't like shoulders but will sit on your lap as you read.

When animals share our homes as pets, we also tend to expect varying degrees of neatness and respect for property. Although proper planning, housing, and socialization can help satisfy this requirement, parrots require high maintenance and a good level of patience when it comes to this issue. Food debris can be contained, soft foods can be cleaned promptly to avoid sticking, and the bird's areas can be modified to minimize the need for heavy cleaning. Sufficient separation from furniture, plants, wood trim, electrical cords, and upholstery is always necessary to avoid possible damage to both pet and objects. In addition, expectations about toilet training should be minimal, even though this is entirely possible in many cases. Realistically, what can be expected from a parrot in respect to toilet training? Your best chance of success resides in your own observational skills and creativity. Most birds will defecate at regular intervals, which gives you some measure of predictability. Most will also show some preferences, in terms of where or in what circumstances they prefer to do it. Simply providing a bird with these circumstances periodically and using praise or a consistent verbal command may accomplish the desired outcome, which is simply to avoid getting soiled. Any type of harsh disapproving behavior, such as yelling or acting upset, should be avoided at all costs. Furthermore, even a bird that "asks" to be allowed to defecate (and many do, by body language or even in plain English) is bound to be somewhat unreliable. If housebreaking your pet is important to you, a dog or a cat will make a much better choice.

Health and Fitness

Although parrots have potentially long life spans, their lives are often cut short due to improper care. Pet cockatiels, for example, can live more than 30 years, but few reach the age of five. Accidents, preventable escapes, injuries caused by children or larger pets, exposure to household chemicals, poor hygiene, and inadequate diet are some of the main causes of premature death.

In addition to shortening the potential life span, improper care reduces the quality of a pet's life. There are many ways to enhance your pet's health and fitness without excessive expense or burden, and you may be surprised to find out that some of these will be good for you and your family as well.

Mature birds tend to look and act very similarly to their younger peers. A healthy parrot should remain active and change little in appearance once it reaches adulthood. Age, however, can make a bird more vulnerable to illness, not only due to the natural aging process, but to the cumulative effects of deficient diets, exposure to toxins, inactivity, inadequate environment, and improper care.

Nutrition

For birds, just as for humans, proper nutrition is very important for health. As we age, the effects of poor diet become more significant because we lose the natural resilience of youth.

In the distant past, pet birds were typically fed a seed-only diet. In addition to boredom, these birds often suffered from vitamin deficiencies, depressed immune systems, and obesity. A seed-only diet is too heavy in fat and too low in calcium and vitamins A and C, just to name a few of its problems. In the wild, most birds eat a variety of available foods, which usually includes green seeds and nuts, fruits and berries, shoots and greens, and animal protein from insects and grubs.

A good commercial food should replicate a bird's natural diet and include nuts, seeds, fruits, and vegetables.

In addition, they must spend a lot of energy locating and accessing these foods, and this activity contributes to their physical fitness.

Today, although the exact nutritional needs of most species are unknown, a great deal of research has resulted in wide availability of commercial pet bird foods. A variety of pelleted diets and many forms of treats are now readily purchased. Catalog companies and pet stores specialize in pet bird goods. Foods such as bean mixes, diced dried fruits, pine nuts in the shell, and other exotic products are now available. However, mature birds that grow up on a seed-only diet may be reluctant to change their habits right away. Furthermore, a drastic change may unnecessarily stress their systems. The best way to change a mature bird's diet is to add new items gradually. After all, there is no need to eliminate seeds altogether, as long as other necessary nutrients are consumed in sufficient amounts.

Because vitamin A and calcium are among the most important nutrients lacking in a seed-only diet, it is a good idea to start by trying to introduce foods rich in them. Many natural foods contain calcium and vitamin A, and if your bird trusts you the easiest way to introduce them is to offer them from your own wholesome meals. You can serve your bird small amounts of your own dinner in a pet dish. Naturally, for this to be an improvement over the previous diet, you must eat these nutritious foods yourself.

We can all benefit from reducing the amount of meat, fat, and salt we consume, and from increasing consumption of whole grains, vegetables, and fruits. Foods that will be good both for you and your bird include sweet potatoes, winter squash, collard greens, kale, corn, brown rice, cooked beans, peas, carrots, salad vegetables (before adding dressing), barley, oatmeal, yogurt, pasta, whole grain breads, nuts, and fruits. Small amounts of lean meat can be offered as well. If you enjoy ethnic foods, the choices are endless. Polenta, quinoa, kasha, amaranth, tofu, sun-dried tomatoes, pine nuts, and sprouts are just some examples of wholesome foods you can share.

If your bird's diet has been inadequate for a long time, it is a good idea to consult your

As in the wild, a healthy diet should be based on a variety of foods; a walnut makes an entertaining and tasty snack for a Goffin's cockatoo.

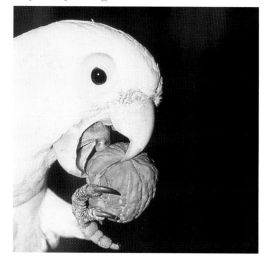

avian vet about vitamin or mineral supplementation. Because some vitamins can build up to toxic levels, it is not advisable to use them without veterinary supervision, particularly if your bird eats commercial pellets or other foods that may already be vitamin-enriched.

A safe way to add some beneficial vitamins and minerals to your bird's diet is to mix a small amount of spirulina in a soft warm meal, such as a cooked breakfast cereal. Spirulina is a natural food sold as a dark green powder. It is an excellent source of beta-carotene and calcium. It is widely used in zoos and in the poultry industry, where it has been found to guard against infection and boost the immune system. Many pet stores and feed stores carry this supplement.

Diseases affect some birds as they age. Budgies, unfortunately, are prone to cancer.

Good nutrition is essential to a mating bird's health; for some birds, calcium supplementation in the form of cuttlebone may be required.

In addition, cuttlebone and mineral blocks may be offered alone or as part of toys as good natural sources of calcium. Dairy products should only be offered in moderation because birds lack the ability to digest lactose. However, a tiny amount of yogurt, cottage cheese, or ice cream, offered as an occasional treat when you are having some yourself, will not cause any problems and will be most appreciated.

A few foods should be avoided. Avocado and persimmons are considered extremely risky. Although not every type of bird tested experienced adverse reactions, some deaths have been reported. With so many safe foods to feed our birds, it certainly makes no sense to test your luck with these. Chocolate, caffeine, and alcohol should also be avoided.

It is a good idea to try to learn as much as possible about the dietary needs of the particular bird in question. As they age, different types of birds exhibit stronger susceptibilities to certain diseases. Many Amazon parrots, for example, tend to become overweight. Some African Greys develop calcium deficiencies. Cockatiels become prone to liver disease. Cancer tends to run in budgies. Whatever your bird, further reading is certain to provide you with much useful information. In addition to books and magazines, electronic resources such as web sites, web newsgroups, and chat rooms are available. Learning from others' experiences may help you avoid—or at least recognize—serious problems before it's too late.

Hygiene

The importance of good hygiene cannot be overemphasized. Proper daily cleaning and good husbandry will prevent health problems for your bird and for you. What is "proper" daily cleaning? Standards do vary, but proper hygiene for pet birds should always involve a thorough daily cleaning that returns all equipment to as good as new condition. This means that cages, toys,

Ruffles

Ruffles is a Timneh African Grey parrot. His age is estimated to be more than 20 years. His present owners have had him for about 14 years, since they rescued him from a bad situation. Ruffles has an open band, indicating that he was imported. His previous owners became frustrated with him because his fear of people resulted in growling and biting. They provided only minimal attention and just enough water, food, and sporadic cleaning to ensure survival. By the time his present owner saw him for the first time, he was in terrible feather condition, his nails were overgrown, and

Ruffles, a Timneh African Grey, was rescued from a terrible existence by a caring new owner.

his beak was soft and deformed due to a serious calcium deficiency. Because his beak condition was beginning to interfere with food intake, he probably would not have lived much longer if he hadn't been rescued immediately.

Ruffles had been fed only sunflower seed mix for at least five years. But after a trip to the vet, some medication and nutritional supplementation, Ruffles started accepting other food items in his new surroundings. Within a year, his beak had grown strong, he had molted into new plumage, and he had begun to trust his new family. Years of patience and good care have turned Ruffles into an affectionate, talkative, beautiful, and healthy pet. Recently, his owners moved into a new home where they can offer Ruffles free flight in a safe situation. This fortunate bird is now "king of the castle" and very happy indeed.

perches, bowls, and other accessories should be completely cleaned of debris, dust, and droppings at least once a day. Bowls should be washed with hot water and detergent or, better yet, washed in a dishwasher. Drinking water should be crystal clear and changed when soiled. Dry foods such as seeds, nuts, pellets, and dry treats may remain in the cage all day, as well as most raw fruits and vegetables. Cooked foods, animal products, or foods with high moisture content should be removed within a couple of hours to avoid excessive bacterial growth, particularly when temperatures are warm. Soiled toys should be washed or, if porous, replaced.

Cage accessories such as perches, toys, and swings must be cleaned on a daily basis of droppings and other debris.

All foods placed in the cage, dry or wet, should be discarded at the end of each day. This is important for nutrition as well as hygiene, because a bird that is fed a large amount of dry food to last several days usually picks through seeds and pellets and eats only its favorite kinds. A bird that is fed a reasonable daily amount, on the other hand, must consume at least some variety, provided that variety is present. Keep in mind that a "reasonable" amount varies for each bird, and that birds must have some food available at all times. Provide just enough food to have a small amount left each day, which will minimize waste and ensure that your bird does not go hungry.

As you can see, proper care involves work and time. Because of this, some bird owners may try to replace a thorough daily routine with a lighter daily procedure followed by weekly thorough sanitizing. This is not a good idea, however; healthy birds have an immune system that allows them to fight modest numbers of bacteria. In normal situations, heavy weekly sanitizing will provide a brief interval of very low bacterial levels, but this will do nothing but expose the pet bird to disinfectants and harsh products. On the other hand, sloppy cleaning during the rest of the week may expose the pet to levels of bacteria that are unmanageable by the bird's immune system. As a bird ages, this becomes increasingly more likely. In addition, poor cleaning exposes the owner and family to higher levels of feather and seed dust. Wet grain residue may grow certain molds that cause diseases in birds and allergies in humans. Dry droppings may disintegrate and become airborne pathogens. Therefore, daily, thorough, and consistent cleaning will be good for you as well as your bird.

There are some situations that may call for even heavier sanitation. Weakened or sick birds may not tolerate bacterial levels achieved with regular cleaning and may require special cleansing products or procedures. Also, if you ever buy used cages or accessories, you will need more than soap and warm water to ensure decontamination. In these cases, a light bleach solution followed by thorough rinsing will usually provide adequate sanitation. Certain products, such as porous

Harmful bacteria can develop quickly in dirty food and water cups.

perches or toys, should not be used by more than one bird, because, just like toothbrushes, they cannot be cleaned enough to be shared safely.

If you live in a warmer climate, rodents and insects may be a problem. Because you can't eliminate the availability of food, and you can't resort to chemicals that may harm your pet, it is often hard to find solutions to these problems. Live traps for rodents are available and usually provide relief. Water dishes placed under each leg of a cage can make effective ant traps. Pesticide-free moth traps for pantries often give good results.

Fortunately, there are many ways to make cleaning easier these days. A hand-held cordless vacuum is a must. Cage aprons funnel debris into the bottom of the cage and contain mess. Sliding trays and grates, full swing doors, dishwasher-safe bowls, and washable portable playpens are some of the many conveniences available today.

Newspaper is a great material for covering the bottom of a tray; it is inexpensive and it permits easy inspection of droppings, toy remains, and food debris, important indicators of a bird's well-being. Layering a few sheets of newspaper on the cage tray also allows for a quick pick-up.

Other tips for quicker cleaning include having two sets of bowls, and feeding soft or messy foods right before cleanup time, in order to easily remove the fresh residue. Keeping the cage over linoleum, tile, or an acrylic pad will help to maintain the cage area in good condition. The position of the perches, food bowls, swings, and other accessories can also impact the amount of cleaning that will be required. Cleaning at night, just before your bird goes to sleep, is most effective. Because your bird won't eat (and usually won't defecate) at night, you can get rid of the evening mess before it takes hold and wake up to a clean cage in the morning. In general, cleaning often, although seemingly time-consuming, is a much more rewarding job than scraping old droppings and dried-out food debris. Both you and your bird will appreciate the results.

Activity and Ergonomic Equipment

The activity level of birds declines somewhat with age. Proper exercise is as important for birds as it is for people, if not more. In the wild, our pet birds would need to fly on a daily basis in search of food. They would have to climb trees, carve nesting cavities, shell nuts, and move around to socialize and play. In captivity, opportunities for these activities are minimal and birds easily become "perch potatoes" once they pass the playful "baby" stage. It is up to the pet owner to encourage enough activity to maintain fitness and health.

The most important piece of equipment you can get to ensure proper activity is a large cage. The biggest cage you can afford and accommodate in your home should work well, provided that the bar spacing is adequate for your particular bird. As a rule of thumb, cage bars should be about one inch apart for Amazons and African Grey parrots. They should be closer together for smaller species and farther apart for larger birds.

Once you have a very large cage, it is easy to set up its interior to promote activity. Different levels and types of perches, several swings, ladders, spiral toys, and food skewers are some of the many strategies to keep birds active. Hanging favorite greens from the top of the cage, placing treats around toys, providing large bathing crocks, and offering nuts in the shell are other ways of enticing even the laziest of parrots to move around.

Observe your bird and look for missed opportunities. Is the cage entirely utilized? If you provide a tall cage and your bird stays in the top section, encourage it to climb down by placing a bowl of treats or a few "foot" toys in a bottom corner. If your bird ignores a swing, hang a new toy or a bell from its top. If carrots are a favorite food, place a fresh carrot with tops on the roof of the cage and let your bird climb for it. If peanuts will entice your bird, place them in a puzzle-box toy.

Some well-intentioned bird owners believe caging provides cruel and unnecessary confinement. As an alternative, they decide to provide their bird with just a playpen or a stand. There are several problems with this approach. First, a cage provides clear territorial boundaries for a pet

Outdoor time—in a secure enclosure—provides fresh air, sunlight, and a welcome change of scenery.

bird. Birds can relax and feel secure in their cages. A bird can experience feelings of comfort and safety in a familiar, roomy, well-equipped cage. Second, although the bird may appear to be less confined, mobility is much more restricted in a playpen than in a cage. A cage with bars, swings, hanging toys, and diverse perches provides many more climbing, playing, and swinging opportunities than a stand. Third, for safety reasons, a bird should be secured when not supervised. Accidents are the leading cause of death in pet birds, and a lone bird prancing around a house is an accident waiting to happen.

Another important way to provide exercise for a parrot is through direct play. Many pet birds enjoy flapping their wings on command, rolling around on a couch, or being chased playfully by their owners. To get my Timneh Eureka to run around happily, all I have to do is say "I'm gonna catch you!" while I jog around her playpen. She loves to escape for awhile and, more than anything, she loves to get caught and kissed once we are both out of breath.

Scarlet

Scarlet is a 16-year-old Green-winged macaw that lives in a pet store. She was raised there, but due to poor socialization and a steep price, she didn't sell as a youngster. At some point, the pet store changed hands and the new owner decided to keep her as the store pet. This bird presented the store with a husbandry challenge because years of improper hygiene had resulted in an unmanageable mess. Perches and cage bars were caked with multiple layers of cemented droppings, toys were no longer recognizable, food and water dishes were in repugnant condition. Scarlet's feathers were beginning to show stress marks, probably as a result of high levels of bacteria and inadequate bathing opportunities.

The new owner and employees replaced the cage and all the accessories. Because Scarlet likes to sit on top of the cage during the day, they strategically placed cat litter pans under her perching spot to catch most

The life of Scarlet, a 16-year-old Green-winged macaw, was greatly improved when new owners took over the pet store where she lived.

droppings. Scarlet is also misted regularly with water and her feathers have since improved. Although her living conditions are still far from optimal, these positive changes have had a noticeable impact on her appearance and mood.

Environmental Stresses

It is a well-known fact that high levels of stress increase vulnerability to illness. Birds, particularly older birds, are very sensitive to stress. Some birds are subject to chronic stress due to family conflict, abuse, neglect, or inadequate protection from children and other pets. Others may experience shorter-lived, sometimes unavoidable stress, due to situations such as home remodeling, parties, overnight guests, changes in family routines, or simply trips to the vet for grooming. As birds age, it is critical to anticipate and reduce stressful situations.

Careful consideration of the cage location is important for reducing stress levels. While considering this, remember that boredom is almost as stressful as discomfort or fear. Ideally, a cage should be placed in an area that affords the bird a good view of interesting activity, as well as an opportunity to retreat to a protected corner. Natural light and views of gardens, birdbaths, or birdfeeders will be appreciated. However, if a bird must endure sun without being able to retreat to shade, or if the cage offers no hideout from scary events, such as a neighbor's cat or a soaring hawk, the problems may outweigh the benefits. Moving the cage partially away from a window, or providing the pet with a bolt-on corner shield or shelter, will reduce stressful situations without depriving the bird of entertainment.

If you are planning a move, a vacation, or another event that may stress your bird, try to minimize the effects ahead of time. Getting a bird used to a boarding cage in familiar surroundings is much easier than in a new place. Giving your bird a chance to get acquainted with a sitter in advance will make your absence more tolerable for your pet.

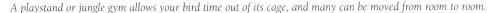

A playstand or jungle gym allows your bird time out of its cage, and many can be moved from room to room.

The cage location should also allow the bird to get enough hours of sleep without disrupting the family schedule. Most parrot species are native to tropical areas, where days and nights last approximately 12 hours each. Because of this, most parrots require about 12 hours of sleep. However, a pet parrot in captivity is likely to nap more during the day than it would be able to in the wild, and this may reduce the necessary hours of night-time sleep. In spite of this, we should allow for a minimum of eight hours of uninterrupted sleep in quiet, and dark or dim light conditions.

Keep in mind that most birds can see quite well with reduce lighting. It is not unusual for them to get startled at night by a nocturnal predator passing by a window, or by moving lights. A

Avery

Special perches and feeding platforms make life easier for Avery, an African Grey without feet.

Avery is a very special African Grey because he has no feet. While his parents were still rearing him in the nest, something upset them and prompted them to bite Avery's toes off. He has a foot stump on one side and a little bit more of a toeless footpad on the other. Most breeders would have thought that Avery had no hope of a quality life and would have destroyed him, but instead lucky Avery was given as a gift to an experienced hand-feeder to give him a chance. His new owner socialized him very well, with a lot of affection, but fostered independence by providing the right environment and equipment. She modified and adapted his cage, providing flat, soft-covered perches and platforms, ramps, low feeding stations, and bolt-on toys. As a result, Avery has no trouble climbing and getting around. He loves food and has become a talented talker. Because he can't use his feet like other parrots, his owner clips his wings in a lighter fashion, allowing him a little flight. Avery is now six years old and looks happy and contented. His special orthopedic condition may give him problems later in life, but for now he can enjoy himself like any loved pet parrot.

low-voltage automatic nightlight placed near the cage will allow a startled bird to get reoriented and to settle back on its perch in such situations.

Birds are creatures of habit and change is stressful to them. However, the personality of your bird and the way in which it is socialized will affect its reaction to change. Some gregarious birds will readily welcome parties, vacations, and car trips. Others will freeze in fear in any unusual circumstance. An older bird's tendencies can be modified with proper guidance and reassurance, but only to a certain extent. We must accept and respect individual differences. This may mean having to protect a bird from "perceived" dangers, no matter how irrational. A bird that learned to fear gloves during capture at a young age may never lose that fear. It would be cruel and pointless to try to force the bird to get used to your gloves.

Observe your bird carefully to learn what events appear to be most disturbing. Any situation that results in thrashing, panicky screams, trembling, or a frozen posture should be avoided or discontinued. When this is not possible, such as during a necessary veterinary exam, talk to your bird calmly and soothingly and provide as much comfort as possible.

Introducing change slowly and in a positive way can make a bird more accepting of new situations. A bird that is put into a car carrier only to go to the vet will naturally be less receptive to travelling than one that regularly goes to picnics at a park.

Birds that have had barren surroundings for years may respond fearfully to new toys. Start with one or two toys of small size and neutral appearance, such as a piece of sisal rope with a knot, or a wooden peg, and a bird may be slowly encouraged to play. By placing these small objects in a bowl, the bird may learn that whatever is placed in there may be fun to play with and gradually accept different things.

Changes in food, cages, toys, or surroundings may upset your bird. Ease such transitions by spending extra time with your feathered friend.

In some cases, birds that were kept for most of their lives in tiny cages will feel unprotected in bigger enclosures. If you have this problem, it is best to introduce a big cage as a play area only. Once the bird is comfortable exploring the cage you may offer a feeding there. Soon after the bird is eating well there, you may try to let the bird spend the night. Once your pet seems happy in its new home, you can retire the old cage. As is the case with other pets and with young children, if you want to provide quality of life and comfort, frequent empathetic observation is your best tool.

Charlie

Charlie, an older Mitred conure, rejected unfamiliar foods and toys until his new owner, with patience and persistence, encouraged him to explore.

Charlie is a Mitred conure of uncertain age. Based on anecdotal history, current condition, and his open band, he is believed to be about 15 years old. Because he had many homes, nobody knows for sure if he was abused or if his terrible fear of hands and anything new is simply an individual trait. Even after spending his last four years with a caring and patient family, his progress in this respect has been limited.

His new owner's first goal was to expand Charlie's menu. Conures need fruits and vegetables, as well as seeds, grains, nuts, and other treats, but Charlie had only been offered wild birdseed for years and wasn't willing to try anything else. With much patience and persistence, and in the presence of other birds that eat a variety of items, Charlie now accepts a few fruits, vegetables, and treats. He is still hand-shy, but now relaxes around familiar people. Charlie's owner also tried to get Charlie to play with toys. Because Charlie looked terrified in the presence of toys, she wove small things through the cage bars, such as pieces of corrugated cardboard, little strands of jute and sisal, crumpled brown paper, and Popsicle sticks. Charlie now plays with these items and is gradually accepting others.

Other environmental stresses should also be considered. Birds have very sensitive respiratory systems and are highly susceptible to air pollutants. Ozone, smoke, sprays, perfumes, and household chemicals pose serious dangers to birds. Sudden deaths of pet birds have been reported and documented from exposure to certain scented candles, fabric deodorizers, some oven bags, and emissions from non-stick cookware. In addition, first-time use of certain appliances, such as heaters and ovens, can also release toxic fumes from the protective coating of heating elements. Although non-stick cookware only emits toxic fumes when overheated, these fumes are usually fatal to birds, and accidental overheating is always a possibility. To be safe, eliminate all non-stick cookware from your house. Watch for this non-stick coating on non-cooking items, such as hair curlers, hotplates, and special light bulbs, and avoid them. Second, minimize the use of household chemicals and use good ventilation when the use is unavoidable. Third, plan construction projects carefully and move your birds out of your house if oil-based paint, smoke, fumes, or strong solvents will be involved. For new carpet installation, unroll and air out the carpet for a few days before bringing it into the house. Fourth, if possible, keep your bird in an air-conditioned room when pollution indexes are high. Fifth, please don't smoke in a bird's home! If you really love your bird, you should try not to smoke at all. This will improve your chances of a long and healthy life together.

Never use the "auto-clean" oven cycle while your bird is in the house. The chemicals released into the air as they are burned off the oven walls can be toxic. It is better for birds and humans alike to use this procedure in good weather and with excellent ventilation.

Joining a pet bird club, subscribing to a pet bird magazine or newsletter, or joining a specialized Internet group are great ways to continue learning about the impact that products may have on your bird's health. These sources are invaluable to remain updated on new product warnings, services, and products.

Stale indoor air and a lack of natural light are other forms of environmental stress. Getting your bird used to a smaller cage to go outdoors with you is a good idea and it comes in handy in emergency evacuations or boarding situations. Supervised, secured birds can spend time outdoors as long as the weather is not too hot or too cold. As a rule of thumb, if you are comfortable in the shade, even when you may need a sweater and light jacket, a healthy bird will be fine. Always protect your bird from direct strong sun, rain, and strong winds, but don't worry about "drafts," because in spite of a popular belief, they pose no real danger. If you can't provide enough natural light exposure due to your climate or living situation, full-spectrum lighting is now readily available.

You can also improve indoor air quality through the use of houseplants. Plants clean the air, reduce indoor pollution, and act as natural humidifiers. For example, a 4-foot hibiscus in a large terracotta planter will consume about one gallon of water a week if placed by a sunny window. In addition to providing welcome greenery and blooms, this dissipated humidity helps maintain feathers, skin, hair, and helps keep breathing passages healthy for the whole family. Because some plants may be toxic, it is understood that plants should not be placed within reach of a bird.

Psychological Wellness

P arrots are intelligent, social animals that need adequate stimulation and emotional bonds to remain healthy. Even when all their physical needs are met, they can fall into a depression or exhibit obsessive-compulsive behavior if left in solitary, barren confinement. These problems may range from transient minor "plucking" or feather picking, to permanent behavioral aberrations, such as self-mutilation. To maintain your pet bird in good psychological condition you must pay attention both to solitary entertainment and social interaction.

How intelligent can a parrot be? You may have heard about the famous African Grey parrot named Alex that has been the subject of Dr. Irene Pepperberg's studies for decades. Alex has been showcased on national television, and in newspapers, magazines, books, and journals. He has a large vocabulary that he uses to identify objects and their properties, such as shape, color, and material. Alex can also count and make comparisons. He is able, for example, to tell which one of two objects is bigger. Alex can also "think" about more than one variable at a time. When presented with a tray of multiple objects of different shapes and colors, he can accurately answer which object is both blue and round, or yellow and made out of wool. Incredible as it may sound, the most amazing things Alex says are of his own creation. He may want to stop a training session by demanding, "Wanna go back! Wanna go chair!" or may express his wishes by requesting, "Want some water" or "Want a nut." Alex has also made up his own words. His word for apple is "bannerry"—as a combination of "banana" and "berry"—and his word for almond is, appropriately, "cork nut."

Dr. Pepperberg's research with Alex has demonstrated that at least this one bird can exhibit

Good food and fun toys are important, but a major part of a parrot's well-being lies in its relationship with its owner.

much more complex cognitive abilities than previously thought possible. Although Alex is the only parrot for which this type of data has been collected and analyzed in a scientific manner, anecdotal evidence from many pet owners suggests that numerous parrots are indeed capable of understanding words and using them appropriately. In addition, many birds exhibit amazing problem-solving skills, particularly when motivated by desire to do something they really want, such as opening their cage, getting food out of puzzle boxes, or tricking their owners into doing what they would like.

On the road to happiness: a well-appointed cage, with perches, toys, dishes, and playstand.

Being more or less intelligent doesn't make a pet more or less deserving of responsible and appropriate care. However, intelligence adds another dimension to the care because the intellectual needs of the pet must be considered. For an intelligent social animal kept as a pet, boredom and isolation is a particularly cruel form of neglect.

Entertainment

Unless your bird has a cage mate, you won't be able to provide your pet with company at all times, so it is always a good idea to pay attention to your bird's available entertainment while alone. Picture yourself in your parrot's cage after you and your family have left home. What is there to do? What is there to look at? What else would you like to have to make your hours of solitude more enjoyable?

Many bird owners decide to get a second bird, but unless you have had your bird for a long time and still continue to enjoy the responsibilities of bird care, it is not a good idea to get a new pet just for this purpose. A second bird will usually require a second cage and double the time and the expense required for good care, actually reducing the time you had for your first pet.

However, if you have an older bird that has never been tame and remains afraid of people, a carefully introduced cage companion of the same species may help. I had this experience many years ago with an older cockatiel that after much patient work was still very reluctant to accept handling. I decided that because he didn't enjoy human companionship enough to be happy, I would get him a cockatiel friend. As a companion, I got him a very tame, people-trusting cockatiel that, instead of making my first bird even less interested in people (as I had suspected might happen), acted as a role model and convinced him to trust humans after all. Even if this had not happened, the addition would have been well worth it for the sake of my first bird's well-being.

Dogs, and more rarely cats, can provide interesting company to a larger parrot. They easily learn that getting too close to the cage often results in a painful nip, so they don't usually present a

Goldie

Goldie is a nine-year-old Blue and Gold macaw that still lives with her first owner, a very responsible and dedicated caretaker. As Goldie grew up, her owner began to appreciate the magnitude of the challenge of coexisting with a macaw in civilized surroundings. Not wanting to give up her home or her pet, she realized that her environment had to be modified to accommodate both Goldie's needs and hers. Large playpens and a huge cage replaced part of the furniture. Swings with baffles were hung from the ceiling. Special areas for feeding soft foods were designed with cleaning and mess containment in mind. Because of these adaptations, Goldie's home still provides the attractive and pleasant surroundings that her owner needs, without unduly confining Goldie or placing unreasonable expectations on her behavior.

Goldie's owner made major adjustments to her home to make life better for the nine-year-old Blue and Gold macaw.

For birds that are reluctant to interact with people, a companion may be a way to break the ice.

danger as long as the bird is secured in the cage or closely supervised.

Depending on your living arrangements, a window, television, or even fish tank may provide some visual stimulation when you are not home. A platform wild bird feeder within window view can be the perfect way of recycling your bird's daily leftovers while providing the entertainment value of the visiting wild birds. In addition to these considerations, there are many other ways to assure proper stimulation for a bird.

Though it is relatively easy to provide some solitary entertainment for a parrot, this is no substitute for social interaction and social play. Talking to your bird while you do your chores, naming treats as you hand them over, and explaining your actions in simple terms (whether your bird understands you or not) are easy ways to interact that don't tax your schedule but do entertain your bird. If you have established trust with your pet, chasing, tickling, rolling over, tumbling, flipping, and gentle wrestling can become

Make life interesting for your bird by providing it with time outdoors or near a window; of course, clipped wings and other security measures should be considered.

favorite games to play with your bird. Many parrots have musical talents and enjoy singing, dancing, and whistling tunes. More intellectually inclined parrots may like training sessions to name colors, numbers, letters, or shapes. In general, what works best for playing with parrots is to follow their lead. The emphasis in their social structure is not on dominance and submissiveness, as it may be in dog packs, but in gentler and subtler exchanges. Besides, these creative clowns often come up with better games than those we humans may invent.

Toys

Toys play a crucial role in a parrot's well-being. The purpose of toys is not to decorate the cage to our taste, but to replace some of the opportunities for natural behaviors that captive birds may be lacking. At the very least, a parrot in the wild would preen (itself and others), shell nuts and fruits, carve cavities, fly, swing on branches, and climb around. These activities can, to a large extent, be replicated at home with the help of toys.

Toys with cotton rope, fabric, sisal, and jute, facilitate preening-type activity and may prevent plucking. Always check these toys for safety because long, strong fibers can cause strangulation and cut circulation in legs or toes. Toys with these materials should have fibers that are short and brittle enough to prevent these accidents. Because these fibers are porous, they should be replaced as soon as they get soiled or wet.

Materials such as wood, raffia, cardboard, leather, cork, and lava rock provide various chewing and carving opportunities. Parrots enjoy the different types and levels of challenge that these objects provide.

Swings, hanging plastic chains, flexible perches, and springing spiral toys can promote exercise

Polly

Polly is a 14-year-old female Double Yellow-headed Amazon. She is a fortunate bird that still lives with her first owner, a truck driver who takes her along on most of her long trips. Over the years, Polly has had to board on many occasions with relatives or friends due to circumstances such as family illnesses or moves, but her life on the road and her loving owner's care have contributed to her adaptability. Polly is in beautiful feather, eats a varied diet, and plays actively. She sings and talks frequently to her owner, who considers her a gentle, affectionate, and rewarding companion.

Polly, a 14-year-old Double Yellow-headed Amazon, frequently travels with her owner, who drives a truck for a living.

and satisfy movement needs. Sounding toys, such as bells, rattles, and music boxes, are enjoyed by most parrots and may stimulate physical activity.

Most "good" toys, from a parrot's point of view, are to be destroyed. This problem can, but doesn't need to, involve considerable expense. Fortunately, for each category of toys you can buy, you can also find recyclable home goods that serve the same purpose. Small empty cardboard boxes filled with corks, short sections of rope with knots, small wooden pieces, and usable portions of partially destroyed toys can provide hours of entertainment for a curious parrot. Pieces of corrugated cardboard or empty paper towel rolls strung through the bars of the cage, crumpled brown paper bags, paper twists, popsicle sticks, wooden clothespins free of metal hardware, and other small objects can provide plenty of free fun as well.

Although inexperienced baby parrots sometimes ingest toy pieces, my avian vet claims that he never treated a mature parrot for ingestion of non-food items. Nevertheless, you should check all objects given to your bird and make sure they are safe and appropriate for your bird's size and strength. This means the toys should not shatter, break into sharp pieces, contain toxic parts, have a strong smell, or appear to have glues, bleeding dyes, or oils. As a rule, offer new types of toys only in supervised play areas, such as playpens, and allow them in the cage only when you are sure your bird will play safely with them when alone. If in doubt, it is better to avoid using a toy altogether than to take a chance.

Cookie

Cookie is an 11-year-old Umbrella cockatoo. While she was still very young, her owner came home to an eerie silence and an empty cage. Following a trail of destroyed baseboard, she located Cookie, alive and kicking, and having a good time. Since that day, Cookie has defied many cage lock mechanisms, but now has one that she can't physically operate. To provide entertainment and satisfy Cookie's lock-picking vocation, her owner provides her with plenty of puzzle toys. Acrylic treat holders, nut feeding boxes, and large sets of nuts and bolts provide the challenge and stimulation that Cookie needs to entertain herself while alone. Her owner believes that this constant supply of interesting toys contributes to Cookie's good nature and well-adjusted behavior.

Cookie, a clever Umbrella cockatoo, needs plenty of challenging and interesting toys to keep her from being destructive.

Your companion bird will appreciate being spoken to—a cheerful "Good morning!" or the names of treats as you hand them over.

Food

In addition to providing proper nutrition, food can be a wonderful entertainment tool. Many commercial parrot diets claim to be "balanced" and discourage owners from providing other foods that may interfere with "perfect" intake. Ask yourself if you would agree to improve your health and life expectancy at the cost of eating just one type of balanced chow. For most humans, the answer to this question is a resounding no. Pet birds, usually deprived of peer company, flight, and freedom, value the pleasures of eating even more than we do. In spite of widespread misinformation about birds' poor sense of taste, any pet bird owner knows that parrots relish a variety of tastes, textures, and temperatures in their meals. A bowl filled with many types of different treats will be a joy to explore and a welcome distraction. In addition, many foods come with their own built-in entertainment. Nuts in the shell, for example, take time and work to be consumed. Depending on the size of your bird, the ideal challenge may be a peanut, almond, walnut, filbert, or Brazil nut. Other entertaining foods include peas in the shell, okra, fresh chili peppers, fresh cranberries, and figs.

Thinking about your bird while you cook dinner can help extend the food pleasures without much trouble. Toast the seeds of winter squashes and melons for special treats. Offer the cores of peppers, the shells of cooked shrimp, an occasional well-cooked chicken bone. Remember your friend and use your imagination. Your thoughtfulness will always be rewarded with excitement and affection.

Play Equipment

In addition to a well-accessorized cage, appropriate equipment spread around other areas of the house can help promote activity and socialization. Nowadays, you can find virtually anything a parrot may want in pet stores, mail-order catalogs, and web sites. If your budget is tight, you can look there for ideas and then build your own versions of play equipment.

A fairly basic need in any parrot household is a playpen. In addition to a cage-top pen, it is a good idea to have a playpen in a different area of the house, or even better, a portable playpen that you can move around. This can give your bird different views of the home, extend the time spent near you, and reduce territorial behavior around the cage. A small dead fruit tree, attached to a base, may make a simple and enjoyable gym. For smaller birds, a folding blanket rack with a few hanging toys may be adequate. Swings and spirals to hang from the ceiling, some with built-in trays and baffles for ceiling protection, are also available. Wherever you decide to use a playpen, pay attention to safety considerations in the surrounding area. Always place the playpen far away from heaters, open water, fireplaces, and other dangers. Remember that even a very calm, wing-clipped bird may get startled by a loud noise and flutter down unexpectedly.

A large crock for bathing opportunities is also a basic need. Although some birds bathe daily and others do it sporadically, all should be able to do it if they wish. If you provide fresh water in a large

Baby

Baby is a seven-year-old Senegal parrot. His owner purchased him from a breeder at a very reduced price because he was a "leftover" bird. Not having sold with the rest of his clutch mates as a baby, he was put back with older birds in the breeder flights for future breeding. When his prospective owner inquired about buying a bird out of season, Baby was brought out and shown to her. Although shy at the time, he was not aggressive. As he settled down in his new home, Baby's love of different foods proved a great tool for taming and training. Within a few weeks, his new owner won his heart with wholesome treats. Soon, Baby expressed affection by regurgitating and even cuddling. Over the years, he has acquired an extensive vocabulary that, although nasal and unclear, he uses in the appropriate context. He has always remained gentle and sweet. His owner feels very fortunate to have given an older bird a chance.

Baby, a gentle and sweet seven-year-old Senegal parrot, was purchased at an older age, but has become a wonderful and treasured pet.

Bathing is an important part of a bird's physical—and even mental—well-being. Provide special crocks for baths or your bird may make due with its drinking water.

heavy dish, at the bottom of the cage, but away from perches and food bowls in order for it to stay clean, your bird will always be able to bathe at will.

If your bird doesn't bathe regularly, you may decide to install a hanging swing in the rear portion of your bathtub or shower stall. Acrylic swings with ceiling protection baffles, plastic chains, and non-porous perches are ideal for this purpose. Although no bird should be placed directly under the shower unless the bird clearly enjoys it, a bird placed within a few feet of the water while you take your shower will benefit from the light misting and vapor.

Behavior Issues

A dopting an older bird is not unlike adopting an older child, in the sense that you avoid some of the troubles of dealing with a baby, but may inherit problems caused by poor early socialization. Fortunately, birds retain their ability to learn, and their behaviors, within limits, may be modified throughout their entire lives.

Screaming

One of the most problematic behaviors parrots may exhibit is screaming. Sometimes, screaming that was previously not problematic becomes problematic due to changes in living conditions. For example, an Amazon parrot that sings loudly in the morning may have been a joy for a family in the country, but may suddenly become a nightmare when the family moves to an apartment in the city. Most often, however, screaming becomes a serious problem when pet owners are generally not very responsive to their bird, but do react when the bird screams. Sometimes, this reaction may involve taking the bird out of the cage, or returning to the room when the bird calls. Naturally, this works for the bird and it reinforces the behavior. In some cases, the owners scream back at the bird, often generating more screaming and providing unpleasant material for the bird to repeat in the future.

If you have a mature bird that screams, there are several things worth trying. Change may come easier than you may think, particularly if you recently acquired a bird with this habit, because both of you will be starting a new relationship on new terms. In any case, the first thing you need to do is to appraise your needs and evaluate the likelihood that they could be met with this particular bird. Setting unrealistic goals will frustrate both you and your pet.

Do you live within earshot of your neighbors? Does someone in your family work third shift, requiring silence during the day? Are you sensitive to noise? If the answer to any of these questions is "yes" your lifestyle may not be suitable for living happily with a parrot. Although screaming

It's natural for parrots to make some loud noises, but problematic screaming may result when a bird feels it is being ignored.

loudly and often is not a necessary evil in each day of a parrot's life, some loud vocalizations or calls on a daily basis should be considered a given. Smaller parrots, such as parakeets, love-birds, or cockatiels, may not have the sound amplification ability of a Moluccan cockatoo, but they also vocalize strongly and often enough to be considered problematic in some circumstances.

What can you realistically expect? Depending on the species, you can expect to reduce loud vocalizations to a couple of brief daily periods, usually in the morning and evening. You can also try to change the nature of the calls, for example, from shrieking demands to happy songs and whistles.

Start by paying more attention to your bird during quiet times. These are the times when we would naturally tend to "let a sleeping dog lie" and ignore our pet, so this will require some discipline on your part. Simply talk to your bird with affection, or provide a treat or a simple toy as a distraction. Respond to your bird's vocalizations, songs, or whistles of appropriate levels. Simply talking or whistling back will do. As your bird gets more attention when quiet, it won't rely on screaming to get it.

When your bird screams, try not to respond immediately, but if you must intervene, don't try to talk above your bird; on the contrary, lower your volume to a whisper.

If you don't know what situations trigger screaming, keep a brief diary to try to deter-mine this. Once you think you may know, do something differently just before you expect the screams to begin. For example, if your bird screams to come out of the cage when you go watch the news, get a portable pen and bring the bird to watch the news with you before screaming starts. If your bird screams in the morning until you get up, try closing the blinds in the bird's room until you get up. If you dis-cover that your bird only screams in certain cir-cumstances, such as when a dog is around, or

If noise control is an issue in your household, consider buying a smaller bird that won't be as loud as a large parrot.

A bird that is kept below your eye level will know that you are in charge; therefore; be careful about allowing your parrot to ride around on your shoulders.

a stranger comes, respect your bird's warning by acknowledging it and providing reassurance.

It is important to try these measures consistently for at least a few months before changing your approach or giving up. Otherwise you will only confuse your bird and make matters worse in the process.

An older or shy bird may need extra time to get used to new toys. African Greys can be especially cautious about change.

Foul Language

Occasionally, an adopted older parrot comes with an undesirable vocabulary that may include rude comments and curses. Funny as this may seem at times, it can be a source of embarrassment and it can interfere with another proper placement, if ever needed. In these cases, a consistent, slightly negative response, such as quietly discontinuing interaction or leaving the room, will often succeed in reducing the undesirable vocalizations. Because any positive reaction, such as increased attention or laughing, is likely to increase the frequency of the vocalizations, the entire household (and even guests) should join in the effort to quell the bird's habit.

Biting

Biting is one of the main reasons owners resell their parrots or give them up for adoption. Obviously, preventing this problem during early socialization is easier than resolving the problem later, but this won't help you if you already have a biting bird. If you had your bird from a young

Samantha

Samantha is an 18-year-old Moluccan cockatoo. She was given up for adoption when she was 14 due to changes in her family. Her previous owners, believing Samantha was a male, called her "Sam" at the time. She lived in a small cage, was given no toys, and ate mainly seed. Her new owners took her to the vet, who determined she was an overweight female, otherwise in good health. With the purchase of a large cage and a few toys, Samantha was stimulated to move around and fruits and vegetables were introduced to her. The most serious problem her new owners faced was loud screaming. This behavior was particularly problematic because Moluccans produce an ear-piercing, deafening call. By paying attention to Samantha before her screaming episodes were anticipated to begin, and by following a predictable routine, her screaming diminished greatly in a relatively short time. She has adapted to her new family and is now an enjoyable, affectionate pet.

Like other Moluccan cockatoos, 18-year-old Samantha was prone to screaming episodes; extra attention from her new family solved the problem.

Although biting is one of the main reasons that birds are given up, there are ways to solve the problem, and even avoid it in the first place.

age and the bird started biting once it matured, you can try to read your bird's body language to predict biting behavior. In some cases, puffed up feathers, a fanned out tail, pinpointing pupils, or sideswiping movements of the head give clear indications of an aggressive mood. In other cases, signs may be subtler, but moods may change according to location in the cage or pen, proximity to a certain toy, or the time of day or year. If you know your bird is going to bite you, it will be good for both of you to avoid this interaction. For this reason, it can be a good idea to "stick train" all birds. This simply means to train them to step up and down from a stick, a tool you can use to move the bird during difficult moments, avoiding an unpleasant confrontation that will make both of you anxious in the future.

Stick training a bird is easy but requires patience. Depending on the size of the bird, you will need approximately two feet of perching material of the appropriate width. This could be a simple dowel. Because many birds are afraid of moving sticks, and are reluctant to accept unsteady footing, you must be careful not to scare your bird. Leaving the stick alone within view of the bird for a few days will be helpful. Once the bird appears relaxed about the stick, place the stick on the floor, and sit down on the floor with your bird. Allow the bird to explore the stick and gently attempt to get the bird to step on it. Do this for a few days, using "up" and "down" as commands, and transferring the bird between the stick and another perch. Once this is accomplished you can use the stick to pick up your bird whenever you think a bite will be likely otherwise.

Much of what has been written about bird training emphasizes controlling the bird at all times. Though it is necessary at times to get the bird to do what we want, when we want to, it isn't always

Stick training, where you use a stick to pick up your bird, is one way of dealing with a bird that bites.

Snapper

Snapper is a Blue-fronted Amazon. Although his age is unknown, his owner has had him for five years. Snapper was sold to him as "unmanageable and vicious," but is now a great pet. Snapper had learned to intimidate his previous owners with threatening postures and bites. As a result, he got what he wanted, which was to stay in his cage, protected from the dogs, cats, and children that ran around wildly. His new owner felt that in such a situation he would have done exactly the same, so he brought Snapper home, provided a new cage in a bright corner within view of a window, toys, and a variety of foods. Although Snapper tried to threaten and bite his new owner the

Blueberries and peanuts, Snapper's favorite treats, were the key to convincing the Blue-fronted Amazon to leave his cage.

first time he took him out of the cage, the owner ignored the bite and proceeded calmly to place him on a playpen where he fed him special treats: blueberries and peanuts. Now Snapper rarely bites and looks forward to all his excursions around his home because he has learned that they will be worth the trip.

necessary to force a bird to comply immediately. Our Red-bellied parrot, Biko, responds well to "advanced notice" commands. For example, if we go to pick him up, and he responds with a threatening posture, we say, "Okay, you are not ready yet…" and let him adjust to the idea. We have learned that just a few seconds later he will follow the command to step up without giving us any trouble. If we are in a hurry, picking him up with a stick is our second option. He accepts the stick without resistance and seems to understand that we cannot wait for him to get ready this time.

In most cases, birds bite only in certain circumstances. If you can avoid those circumstances, you have solved your problem. Older, wild-caught birds, may never learn to accept hands, but may step up on an arm, accept a tickle on the head, or give a kiss. Respect the limits set by your bird and move slowly in this area. Forcing unwelcome physical interaction is nothing but a form of assault.

As previously explained, when mature birds regurgitate they are expressing affection. When this behavior is brief and performed in greeting, it usually poses no problem. However, more prolonged and increasingly effusive regurgitation is usually more characteristic of a courtship ritual. This type of behavior should be discouraged because it can escalate into frustration and aggression. This usually happens when a bird relates to a human as a mate and doesn't get the desired response. If you notice that your mature bird does this when you wear a given garment, pet the bird in certain way, or play with a particular toy, it is best to avoid the situation. If you can't identify a trigger, you may simply return the bird to the perch or cage for a few minutes and offer a distraction, such as a treat or a small toy. Some of the objects that may trigger courtship or nesting rituals in mature birds are boxes, tissues, rags, bells, and mirrors. In general, anything that may resemble a nesting

Feather plucking, which is especially common in African Greys, can be the result of a physical condition, nutritional deficiency, or a lack of stimulation.

site or nesting material has the potential to arouse these tendencies. These objects don't have to be completely avoided with all birds, but each bird's reactions should be watched.

Some birds bite because of uncontrollable fear. Because pet birds have been bred in captivity only recently, many older birds are wild caught and still retain a natural fear of people. These birds can make good pets if we respect their individuality and adjust our expectations. They may never cuddle or become completely hand-tame, but they may reward our loving care with an increasingly contented and calm disposition. Many of these birds (some of them retired breeders) are in need of good homes.

Gorky

Gorky, a 12-year-old Congo African Grey, plucks her feathers less now that her new owners can spend more time with her.

Gorky is a 12-year-old female African Grey parrot. Her present owners adopted her when she was about two years old. Her first owner didn't have enough time to spend with her and she had started to pick her chest feathers.

Like many African Greys, Gorky is a very good talker. She knows all her family members by name, requests treats appropriately, and refers to daily routines in context. She is fortunate to live in a household where there are other pet birds, and where all pet birds are considered members of the family. Gorky receives plenty of human attention and affection, in addition to proper care and diet. Her feather-picking tendency has improved significantly. It is now reduced to very mild, seasonal over-preening in spring, during the normal molt.

Feather Picking

Over-preening, feather picking, feather plucking, and self-mutilation are varying degrees of the same problem. Natural preening sometimes continues obsessively, resulting in abnormal behavior. In the wild, birds preen their mates, offspring, and other flock members in addition to themselves. In captivity, these opportunities are missing. Boredom and other stresses may also increase the propensity to over-preen.

Some parrot species, like African Greys and cockatoos, are particularly prone to this problem, which is somewhat rare in Amazons. However, any type of pet bird can exhibit this behavior. Once this habit is well established it is difficult to break, but a few things are worth trying.

First, a veterinary exam should rule out a physical condition, because certain infections, nutritional problems, systemic diseases, and toxicities may result in feather picking. Second, be

Pio

Pio is a female cockatiel. Her owner received her as a gift about 12 years ago. Although Pio was quite tame at the time, her owner had never handled a bird and was afraid of beaks and toenails. Because of these fears, she never took Pio out of her cage. But her owner provided Pio with an ample cage, meticulous cleaning, a variety of foods, and plenty of companionship, so Pio continued to get head scratches and stayed tame.

A few years later, the owner's granddaughter took an interest in the bird. She decided to adopt her, but she wanted to play more actively with her. Pio was very afraid to come out of the cage; she had become cage-bound. In this case, the previous owner suggested that switching the cage with a new, unfamiliar one could help her granddaughter with her goal. This strategy worked. Because Pio had to choose between a familiar person and an unfamiliar cage, she felt more comfortable playing with the

It didn't take long for Pio, an older cockatiel that had become cage bound, to leave her cage for playtime with her new owner.

granddaughter, taking food from her, and riding on her shoulder. By the time she became familiar with the new cage, the new routines were well established and continue to be part of her new life.

certain that your bird's diet is appropriate, interesting, and varied. Third, provide enough attention and opportunities for play. Toys that may be helpful in curbing this behavior are those of the "preening" type, such as cotton rope, sisal, leather, fabric, and jute. Chewing toys made out of soft wood, cardboard, cork, and straw may offer distraction and reduce the time spent on the behavior. Opportunities for bathing and an adequate level of humidity are also important. Gentle misting with water on a regular basis may be helpful.

If, in spite of all these measures, your bird continues to pick or pluck feathers, you may have to accept some of this. However, self-mutilation is a more serious problem and it may require the use of a collar under veterinary supervision. Before deciding on a particular course of action, a complete veterinary exam is always advisable in any case of feather picking or self-mutilation.

Frustrating as this problem may be for the conscientious pet owner, a feather-plucked older bird may be well worth adopting. Once the obvious causes are ruled out, a funny appearance is the only consequence of this behavior, and with long-term proper care this may even improve some day.

Cage Binding

Another behavioral problem that new owners of adopted birds may encounter is cage binding. This behavior can be best described as an abnormal attachment to a cage that may result in clinging to the cage, refusal to come out of it, or aggressive territorial protection of the cage area.

Cage binding is common in older birds that were confined to a cage day after day. In many of these cases they have received no comfort other than the food received there and the sense of safety provided by the enclosure.

Some gentle encouragement and patience may be all it takes to convince a hesitant bird to leave its cage.

Though pet owners may not consider cage binding a problem, particularly if they don't want to spend time supervising their pet outside of the cage, it interferes with the bond that pet birds and owners can develop in less restricted circumstances.

There are many ways of addressing this problem, but all involve time and patience. In some cases, when birds have been the victims of physical abuse, owners may simply have to accept the bird's limitations and adjust their expectations. In most cases, however, this behavior can be slowly changed. You may try opening the door of the cage and gradually tempting the bird out with special treats or toys. If the bird starts accepting this routine, you may increase the distance between the cage and the play area. In some cases, moving the bird around in the cage may be helpful. Whatever you do, never become impatient with a bird that clings to its cage for safety; you want your bird to consider you as a protector and not an enemy.

Veterinary Care

As birds age, veterinary care becomes both more necessary and more risky. Preventing health problems by reducing exposure to pathogens and stress is as important as detecting health problems before they become too severe. Unfortunately, a vet's office can expose birds to both pathogens and stress. At the same time, it can save your bird's life. Because birds hide signs of disease until late in the course of an illness, wasting time in decision making can prove fatal. When in doubt, you should always consult an avian vet. A true avian vet has both significant experience treating birds and significant knowledge necessary for certification. In addition, the "bedside manners" of avian vets tend to be more bird-friendly due to handling skills acquired through practice. Avian vets also have the appropriate equipment and tools required for proper bird exams and interventions. These specialists' fees are often the same as any other vet's, but their service gives birds their best chance for a solution to their problems.

In order to provide the most responsible care while avoiding unnecessary visits to the vet's office, you should monitor your bird for a few indicators on a daily basis. An important characteristic of good health is a steady body weight. If you handle your bird, you will be able to notice subtle weight changes. If you are not good at this, or if you don't handle your bird much, get a scale and use it weekly, preferably at the same time of day.

Frequent handling of your bird will prepare it for the inevitable visits to the vet; you'll also be able monitor any weight changes.

Another important indicator of well-being is consistent food intake. If your bird seems to be eating a lot less, a lot more, or consuming much more water than usual, an avian vet consultation is in order.

The appearance, size, and number of droppings can also be very telling. A normal bird dropping has a brownish-green formed part (stool), a clear watery part (urine) and a whitish stain (urates). The stool portion is the most variable one, often changing color depending on the food intake. Beets can predictably result in red stools. Carrots or papaya can give an orange tint. Blueberries or blackberries may produce purple droppings. A change in brand of pelleted diet can also change the color of the droppings. The urine portion may be more voluminous under stress, but it should continue to be clear. Very small or dry droppings may indicate dehydration or poor food intake. Colored urine may indicate liver disease. Watery stools may be due to bacterial infection. A careful daily check of the lining of the cage as you replace it is well worth the effort. Any drastic changes justify a visit to the vet.

Feather condition is a good indicator of health—feathers should be sleek and clean.

Feather condition should appear good, even through normal molts, and activity level should be more or less constant from day to day. However, some very ill birds may still show perfect feathers.

Breathing should be almost imperceptible. If you notice any laboring, significant chest expansion, open beak breathing, panting, or tail bobbing, your bird needs immediate veterinary consultation.

If any condition suggests the need for a visit to the vet, don't delay. Try to book the first morning appointment, so the vet's office will be as sterile as possible. Bring your own towel to ensure that no other bird has been in contact with it. Handle your bird yourself as much

Trips to the vet can be especially traumatic for those birds not accustomed to being in a travel carrier.

as possible during toweling and restraining to reduce stress. Your bird won't like to be toweled by you anymore than by the vet, but it will feel less threatened. And remember that you know your bird better than anyone else, so don't be afraid to be assertive and offer suggestions that may improve your pet's comfort during examinations and treatments.

Beak trimming or buffing is a difficult grooming task that should only be done by an avian veterinarian.

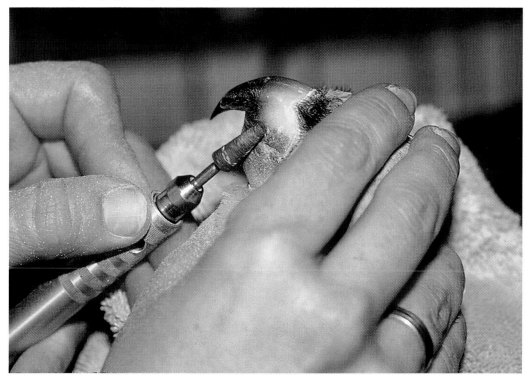

Routine Care

In addition to adequate nutrition, good husbandry, fresh air, exercise, and social stimulation, routine proper care requires grooming. Necessary grooming includes feather clipping and toenail clipping. In rare circumstances, a beak may need filing or repair, but this is usually as a result of innate deformity, injury, or disease. Only avian vets should be allowed to perform beak-grooming procedures. For a parrot, the beak is a vital structure essential for proper food intake. In addition, it has a blood supply and many nerves, making any intervention both painful and risky. Needless to say, beak injuries are serious and require immediate attention.

Once understood, wing clipping is a very simple, painless procedure. However, improper clipping can cause permanent injury and severe bleeding; under-clipping can result in escape, and over-clipping can result in crash landings. Because of this, it is important to observe an experienced person demonstrating the proper procedure before attempting it yourself. In addition, different types of birds may require different clippings. A streamlined strong flyer will need a more drastic clipping than a plump bird. Clipping more feathers to be "on the safe side" is not always a wise idea because a bird without enough wing surface has no ability to glide down gently and may fall down too harshly, getting injured in the process.

Generally, proper clipping involves cutting some of the primary flight feathers just below the tips of the primary coverts (the layer of feathers that covers part of the primaries). Usually, by cutting below this line, you will avoid cutting "blood" feathers, those still growing with an active blood supply. The number of primaries to be cut depends on the bird, but it may range from as few as four or five to all the primaries.

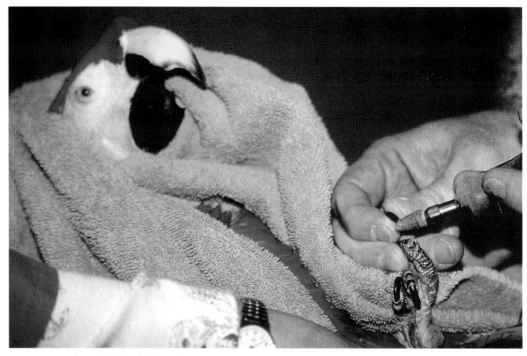

Routine care of most birds includes nail trimming when required.

Cutting a blood feather may result in serious blood loss. If this happens, the cut feather usually has to be plucked out to stop the bleeding. It is easy to recognize blood feathers by their appearance in the underside of the wing. At the base, each blood feather is covered by a thick waxy tube. This tube protects the blood supply and rarely extends below the end of the primary coverts.

Some pet bird owners question the need for wing clipping. Certainly, flight is an important natural activity for birds that should not be prevented without careful consideration. However, many pet birds bred in captivity have not learned to navigate safely. In these circumstances, flying indoors becomes dangerous. In addition, a survey of "lost-and-found" ads in any local paper will provide sad confirmation that many pet birds simply fly away. In most cases, the birds don't know how to return, even though they may try. Virtually every lost bird becomes a victim of predators, exposure, or other traumatic loss.

For some birds, a special pedicure perch may be all that is needed to maintain proper nail length.

Toenail grooming is a little more involved than wing clipping. Special scissors are available for this purpose, but tiny nail clippers can also be used. Just the very tips of the nails should be removed, and only if they are so sharp that they tangle easily in clothing or toy parts. Cutting more than just the tip could cause bleeding, pain, and possibly permanent injury. In addition, your bird may be deprived of enough grip to climb safely around the cage.

Before attempting any grooming procedures, be completely certain that you know what you are doing, get help to restrain the bird appropriately as needed, and have a jar of styptic powder at hand, in case you cause any bleeding and need to stop it.

Many products are available these days to minimize the need for nail clipping. Cement perches, swings, and hanging toys provide the necessary wear for toenails to remain blunt. In addition, perches of different types and diameters promote foot health and facilitate proper foot posture and grip, which will contribute to nail health.

The importance of foot care for older birds cannot be overemphasized. Pet birds spend

Although wing clipping is fairly simple, a new owner should always watch someone with experience before attempting it alone.

their entire lives on their feet, unlike mammals, which sit and lie down. A nice variety of perching surfaces should be available to birds at all times. Ideally, a cage should have soft perches, such as rope or sisal, some type of flat platform perch, natural wooden perches of varying widths, and cement perches or swings.

Those birds used to being handled, whether with gloves or a towel, will be more at ease with the grooming process.

An older bird's feet may need a break from constant perching, so allow your bird time on different—but safe—surfaces and platforms.

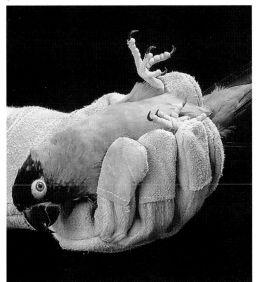

Special Geriatric Concerns

What is a "geriatric" bird? Opinions vary greatly. Depending on the species and the type of care received throughout their lives, birds can appear youthful and exhibit good appearance into very advanced years. Because captive breeding is a relatively recent practice, some of the oldest birds we come across tend to be wild–caught imports of uncertain age. Most breeders and avian vets will be able to say that they have seen an Amazon that was "at least 40" or a Grey that was "at least 50," but the truth is that it is rare to find many birds in those age ranges. As a result, our knowledge of birds' advanced age problems is limited and based on case studies and anecdotes. No large-scale studies of older parrot populations in captivity are available at this point.

In addition to the problem of age verification, birds, like people, present great individual variation in the ways they age. Genetics, as well as environment, plays an important role. Long-term studies of large numbers of birds of the same species, living in controlled conditions, would be necessary to draw clear and certain conclusions about their aging patterns.

Most parrot breeders report no special problems with their older breeder birds. Some report that hens believed to be quite old may stop laying eggs or begin laying soft-shelled eggs. This problem, sometimes seen as a result of lower calcium levels, can lead to egg binding. However, many breeders report keeping old parrot hens in good condition long after they have stopped laying eggs and producing young.

Older birds should still be active, but they may appreciate perches and toys placed lower to the ground.

Foot problems seem to be a relatively common ailment of mature birds. Most of these problems start as a result of improper nail grooming and inadequate perches. Although improvement is almost always possible, if these problems have been longstanding they may have caused permanent deformities. A careful veterinary assessment of foot condition and the optimal nail grooming are essential first steps. A variety of perches should follow, including soft (cotton or sisal) and hard (wood and cement) surfaces of various shapes and diameters. A corner platform, a shelf, or a flat square perch can provide a welcome rest to tired feet. Any bird with foot problems should also have a soft-covered flat platform, such as a small carpeted area.

Keep in mind that birds may forego the luxury of foot comfort in exchange for a feeling of security. This means that if you offer a comfortable perch in a location that makes the bird feel vulnerable, your bird may opt to sleep on another perch at the expense of physical discomfort. Observe the location your bird seeks to relax and nap. This is usually a high corner of the cage that provides some visual shelter. Try to provide comfortable, ergonomic perching options there for maximum benefit.

Rope and pedicure perches of differing diameters may help a mature bird with developing foot problems.

As a bird ages, mobility may suffer due to aches and pains, slower reaction time, or impaired perception. Cataracts, for example, may reduce vision, causing "false" steps. If you notice gradual changes in mobility in an old but otherwise healthy bird, take a careful look at the cage and provide thoughtful adjustments. You may lower the food bowls, hang a heavy toy from each side of a swing to make it more stable, add a climbing rope between two points to facilitate access or to break an accidental fall.

There have been reported cases of parrots that have become seemingly "senile" in old age. A thorough vet exam may be particularly helpful in these cases, because what appears to be "senile" behavior may have another root cause, such as pain, deafness, or blindness. A complete assessment is essential to design adaptations or to decide what's best for the bird's quality of life in the future.

In general, appearance changes little as a parrot ages. The feet may become scalier and somewhat knobby, the beak and nails may

Food and water bowls can be lowered to accommodate birds that have reduced mobility or impaired eyesight.

develop a thicker, less lustrous look. The areas around the eyes may become a bit more wrinkled, and the skin covering the nostrils may thicken. Feathers may look a little "rattier" but should remain relatively attractive as long as the bird is healthy. Some green feathers may change to yellow or black. This can be similar to humans' hair graying process, but it is some times a result of nutritional deficits and should be assessed by an avian vet. In general, no drastic changes should be attributed to normal aging until other possible causes have been ruled out.

Only recently has the field of avian medicine flourished. Not many years ago, it would have been difficult, if not impossible, to find a vet that would even attempt to treat birds. Recent developments in general medicine, such as microsurgery, laser surgery, chromosomal analysis, and highly sensitive tests developed to detect sub-clinical viral and bacterial infections have helped advance avian medicine at an unprecedented rate.

Final Thoughts

Humans have kept birds as pets for centuries, but today this privilege presents us with a special challenge. As entire wild populations of parrots have been wiped out due to environmental degradation and trapping, newly available pet parrots come almost entirely from domestic production. Knowledge and experience continue to increase the success rates of captive breeding, baby parrots have become abundantly available in the market, and prices have begun to fall. The appeal of baby parrots makes them an easy sell, contributing to an emerging predominance of uninformed impulse purchases. Many of these birds are fortunate enough to end up with responsible families that learn along the way and make the necessary adjustments that life with a parrot will demand for a long time. Many more, however, disappoint their unprepared owners and join the precarious ranks of unwanted pets. Sanctuaries, adoption programs, and foster homes are already becoming overcrowded with these unwanted birds.

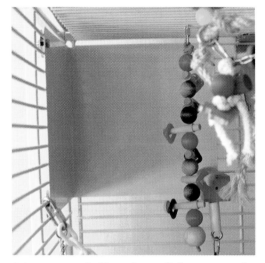

Bolt-on privacy shields can be installed in a corner of a cage for those birds that may need more of a sense of security.

It is my hope that this book will help you renew your commitment to an older, perhaps "less-than-perfect" pet bird, or consider providing a home to one in desperate need. There are approximately 330 species of parrots in the world today and about one–third of these species are endangered or threatened due to loss of habitat or capture. Those of us fortunate enough to share our time with a companion parrot should fully appreciate this priceless gift. We should embrace the responsibility of providing them with good care, respect, and affection. We should accept them as they are, discover their uniqueness, and marvel at them.

Because our birds may outlive us, our responsibility for our pets' well-being extends beyond the direct care we can provide. We should avoid the trap of making them fit the mold of the "perfect pet," while gently guiding and promoting "acceptable" behaviors. Our pet may some day need to adjust to a new home. A bird that has been loved and treated with dignity will be better equipped to gain affection, to adapt to a new situation and to establish new bonds. A properly socialized pet bird will be more easily welcomed and accepted by a new household, and so your good care will continue to comfort your bird, even in your absence.

Author Delia Berlin with husband David, Timneh Eureka, and Red-bellied parrot Biko.

Resources

AFA Watchbird

American Federation of Aviculture, Inc.
P.O. Box 56218
Phoenix, AZ 85079
www.afa.birds.org
The AFA is a nonprofit organization dedicated to the promotion of aviculture and the conservation of avian wildlife through the encouragement of captive breeding programs, scientific research, and the education of the general public. The AFA publishes a bi-monthly magazine called *AFA Watchbird*.

Association of Avian Veterinarians

P.O. Box 811720
Boca Raton, FL 33481
561-393-8901
561-393-8902
www.aav.org
AAV membership is comprised of veterinarians from private practice, zoos, universities and industry, veterinary educators, researchers and technicians, and veterinary students. Serves as resource for bird owners who are looking for certified avian veterinarians.

Bird Talk

Subscription Dept.
P.O. Box 57347
Boulder, CO 80323
www.animalnetwork.com
Bird Talk is a monthly magazine noted for its directory of avian breeders, as well as its species profiles and informative articles and columns on health care and behavior.

Bird Times

Pet Publishing, Inc.
7-L Dundas Circle
Greensboro, NC 27407
www.birdtimes.com
Bird Times magazine is a source of entertaining and authoritative information about birds. Articles include bird breed profiles, medical reports, training advice, bird puzzles, and stories about special birds.

The Gabriel Foundation

P.O. Box 11477
Aspen, CO 81612
www.thegabrielfoundation.org
A nonprofit organization promoting education, rescue, adoption, and sanctuary for parrots.

The NAPS Journal

North American Parrot Society, Inc.
P.O. Box 404
Salem, OH 44460
www.drzoolittle.com
Formed in 1995, NAPS sponsors bird shows and aims to put fun back into showing for exhibitors. NAPS members are individual pet owners, breeders with small and large aviaries, show judges, veterinarians, and people who enjoy exhibiting. Members can purchase closed bands from NAPS.

Index

Photo Credits

Glen S. Axelrod, 8

Joan Balzarini, 4, 10T, 15B, 26, 32T, 38, 40B, 41T, 44T, 47, 52, 53B, 60T, 61T

Delia Berlin, 10B, 12, 18, 19, 21, 23, 24, 25, 30B, 31, 32B, 33, 34, 36, 37, 44B, 45, 46, 48, 53T, 56B, 57BR, 60B, 62

Isabelle Francais, 1, 14, 15T, 16T, 17T, 22, 35, 40T, 57T, 57BL, 58

Michael Gilroy, 17B

Eric Ilasenko, 41B, 50, 54

Robert Pearcy, 30T

John Tyson, 6, 11, 28, 42, 56T